AF488409

Disclaimer:

The information provided in this book about financial literacy is for general informational purposes only. It is not intended to be a substitute for professional financial advice, and readers should consult with a qualified financial advisor or expert before making any financial decisions.

The author and publisher of this book have made reasonable efforts to ensure that the information contained herein is accurate and up-to-date at the time of publication. However, they make no representations or warranties of any kind, express or implied, about the completeness, accuracy, reliability, suitability, or availability with respect to the information, products, services, or related graphics contained in this book for any purpose.

The author and publisher shall not be held responsible or liable for any loss or damage, including but not limited to financial loss, indirect or consequential loss or damage, or any loss or damage arising from the use of this book or the information contained herein.

The inclusion of any links, references, or recommendations in this book does not necessarily imply a recommendation or endorsement of the views expressed within them. The author and publisher have no control over the nature, content, and availability of those sites or resources.

Every individual's financial situation is unique, and the strategies, concepts, and advice provided in this book may not be suitable for everyone. Readers are encouraged to exercise their own judgment and discretion when applying the principles discussed in this book to their personal financial circumstances.

The reader assumes full responsibility for any actions taken based on the information provided in this book. The author and publisher disclaim any liability or responsibility for any consequences or outcomes, whether positive or negative, resulting directly or indirectly from the use or application of the information in this book.

It is important to note that financial markets and regulations can change rapidly. Therefore, readers should independently verify any information before making financial decisions or taking any action.

By reading this book, the reader acknowledges and agrees to the above disclaimers and releases the author and publisher from any liability or responsibility arising from the use or reliance on the information provided in this book.

What
is
Money?

Money is a currency that is used in payments to buy items and services. There are two main forms of money: physical money and digital money. Physical money comes in the form of dollar bills and coins, while digital money consists of debit and credit cards.

When you use a debit card, it uses the money that is in your bank account. HOWEVER, when you use a credit card, it uses the bank's money.

When you borrow the banks money, you have to pay them back on time.

If you do not pay the bank back on time, they charge you extra money in ADDITION to what you already owe them.

This is called Interest!

Everytime you use a credit card you earn REWARDS!

For example, if I use my credit card at the store to buy a $10 item, the bank will give me a reward of 1-3% of that $10 for using their money instead of my own. HOWEVER, you still have to pay the bank back their $10 on time.

Ways to Make Money...

There are several ways to make money and you are not limited to one way at all.

One way to make money is by getting a job.

There are various types of jobs you can have such as babysitting, dog walking, or working at a restaurant.

Some jobs require experience, while others don't. However, jobs are **NOT** the only way to make money.

Another way to make money is to be self-employed; this means you work for YOURSELF. You create a business and you work for that business. Examples include being a barber, Hairstylist, Private Chef, a driver or Private Security.

Lastly, You can be a Business owner. The difference between being a business owner and being self-employed is that you are not trading your time for

MONEY.

This means even when you are not working, your business is still paying you.

For example: A restaurant owner will earn money as long as their restaurant is open. Regardless of if they are there or not.

Ways to Save Money...

As you earn money it is also important to save. There are a few ways to save your money including: savings accounts, piggy banks, and mutual funds.

A savings account
is a designated account that is
in your bank account specifically
made for you to save your
money. Most banks will give you
around .01% Interest
on your money annually. This
is close to nothing, but a
Savings account can be
useful to set aside money.

A piggy bank can come in all shapes and forms. It can be an actual piggy bank, it can be a shoe box, under the mattress, a drawer, a SOCK, whatever you wish it to be. This option gives you 0% interest on your money.

Lastly, a mutual fund is a large stock that has a lot of the big companies in it.

With stocks there are always RISKS. But mutual funds are low risk stocks and in the last 10 years they have increased 8-12% on average.

How to Invest your Money...

When you make money, you want it to grow. While saving money is beneficial, it is also important to be aware of inflation.
INFLATION is the depreciation of money over time.

When you invest you want to be smart; Have your parents do research or talk to their financial advisor to educate you on how to invest correctly. One way to invest is in stocks. There are many different stocks out there. Owning a stock is like owning a piece of that company. So Let's say you own 1 share of an Apple stock. Every time Apple makes money, you make money.

Although investing allows you to make money, there are also risks. This is why it is important to make smart decisions and consider the risks prior to investing.

There are also lower-risk stocks called exchange traded funds, or ETF's. An ETF is one BIG stock that has a lot of companies inside. So, if one company does Bad it does'nt impact you as much.

Additionally, custodial accounts are a safe way to start investing while under the age of 18. A custodial account is an investment account for minors that is ran and managed by the legal guardian. With this account, your guardian can invest into stocks for you until you are of legal age.

In conclusion, there are various ways for you to earn, save, and invest your money. I hope you take away some of the fundamentals of FINANCIAL LITERACY and continue to educate yourself on smart ways to use your money so it grows over time.
BARBER
HAIR SALON

Hello I am your author, Julio Ayamel.
I wrote this book because I knew nothing about financial literacy growing up. In fact, I didn't even know that stocks existed until my sophomore year of high school. I wanted to educate and empower other individuals like myself about the basics of financial literacy and how you can get ahead of the game with saving and investing. I encourage you to start asking questions and doing your own research on the topics discussed in this book so you can start your journey to becoming more financially literate.
God bless!